SEASON OF CAROLS

ISBN 0-634-06803-2

7777 W. BLUEMOUND RD. P.O. BOX 13819 MILWAUKEE, WI 53213

Visit Hal Leonard Online at
www.halleonard.com

Forward and Performance Notes

The idea behind the creation of these arrangements is to provide music that would be performable by student musicians who have studied string instruments for at least one year. Equally important is to provide interesting high quality arrangements of popular traditional holiday songs with a level of musical sophistication not often found in student literature. This effort has resulted in material that could be programmed by string orchestra groups of any level as well.

Each piece has challenges which align with studies and techniques a student player encounters in popular second and third year string educational programs.

• FINGERINGS:

All of the violin and viola parts can be performed in 1st position, if needed, by students at these levels. I have marked many 1st position fingerings as helpful reminders for the student, and as aids to the teacher. At times the cello parts and often the bass parts require shifts to other positions, as students of these instruments learn shifts earlier than the violinists.

• BOWINGS:

The bowings have been marked as a starting point, and to a certain extent, take into consideration the young students' lesser bow control. There are, of course, other possibilities for bowings depending on the ability of the players and the desired musical result.

• OPTIONAL PARTS:

I have included optional harp, piano, and percussion parts. These parts are not required for a complete performance, however, they do have a significant beneficial effect on the sound of the pieces.

The harp parts, (not merely rewritten piano parts), were written with the harpist specifically in mind. The harp parts are "full" to help account for deficiencies in numbers of the lower strings, should that be the case with a given group. They were written with the student in mind, however, student harps with various limitations of range and chromatic possibilities have not been addressed. That is not to say though that the parts are unusable for the more limited instruments. For the most part, the parts are easily adaptable to the capabilities of the student and his/her instrument.

The piano parts are the most utilitarian of the optional parts. They should be used, at the conductor's discretion, if the harp is not available, and only to fill out what might be weak or missing from the string family. The conductor and pianist are given the license to edit or eliminate anything that is redundant for their group. Please see the notes on the harp and piano parts for instrumentation preferences.

The percussion parts, playable by one or more players, are simply a nice addition to have.

3rd Violin parts as substitutes or additions to viola parts are also included. In some cases, compromises have been made to the voicing of the music to accommodate range. Needless to say, these parts should be used with discretion when necessary to fill the void created by missing violas.

• POSSIBILITIES FOR PEDAGOGY:

All of the pieces contain the opportunity to explore dynamics. They also have harmonic content that is a bit sophisticated and, in that way, can be opportunities to focus on intonation.

"Away In The Manger" – Legato bowing and bow control. The "C" string on the cello.

"Chanukah, Oy Chanukah" – Pizzicato – easy optional double stops – bowing.

"Deck The Hall" – Bow lifts – playing off the string – marcato.

"Ding Dong! Merrily On High!" – "Bell tones" forte-piano – staccato – intonation – independent parts.

"Greensleeves" – An opportunity for a violin soloist, optional shift at the end. Optional solo cello with shifts. Legato bowing – optional easy tremolo (violins) – expression – balance – independent parts.

"God Rest Ye Merry, Gentlemen" – Tempo changes – following the conductor.

"O Come, All Ye Faithful" – More interesting and challenging viola part – dynamics – slightly chromatic cello/bass parts.

"O Holy Night" – Bowing – simple duplets in 6/8 – slightly chromatic cello/bass parts.

"Pat-A-Pan" – Probably the most challenging piece in the collection - open string pizzicato – key of G minor introduces B♭ and E♭ – Key change to A minor – optional solos for violin, viola, cello – independent parts.

"Silent Night" – Optional easy single note harmonics (2nd harmonic) for cello, viola, 2nd violin – more featured harp part – short optional solos – some chromatic harmony.

"Three Holiday Songs" – Tutti pizzicato section can be bowed if desired.

"We Wish You A Merry Christmas" – "Bell tones" forte-piano – independent parts in a fugal section - key change from G major to D major.

– Bruce Healey

AWAY IN A MANGER

Traditional
Arranged by BRUCE HEALEY

* Violin 3 (Viola T.C.) part included though not shown on the score.

04490308

4
Vln. 1
Vln. 2
Vla.
Cello
Bass
Harp
Piano
Perc.
hi3
hi4
hi3
hi3
hi3
mf
mf
Ped.
Ped.
Mark Tree
17
18
19
20
21
22
23 p
24
Vln. 1
Vln. 2
Vla.
Cello
Bass
Harp
Piano
Perc.
hi2
hi2
hi3
mf
mf
mf
8va
8va
lift
Ped.
Ped.
Ped.
Ped.
Triangle
Mark Tree
24 mf
25
26
27
28
29
30
31 p
04490308

5
04490308
32
Vln. 1
Vln. 2
Vla.
Cello
Bass
Harp
Piano
Perc.
Triangle
8va
Ped.
Ped.
Ped.
hi2
hi2
mf
32
33
34
35
36
37
38
Poco rit.
41
Rit.
Vln. 1
Vln. 2
Vla.
Cello
Bass
Harp
Piano
Perc.
Mark Tree
Triangle
hi2
hi2
hi3
hi3
hi3
hi3
p
p
p
p
dim.
dim.
dim.
p
p
Ped.
Ped.
39 p
40
41
42
43
44
45 p
46 pp

DECK THE HALL

* Violin 3 (Viola T.C.) part included though not shown on the score.

Vln. 1
Vln. 2
Vla.
Cello
Bass
Harp
Piano
Perc.
f marcato
lift
lift
lift
lift
lift
lift
on the string
p
lol 1

Vln. 1
Vln. 2
Vla.
Cello
Bass
Harp
Piano
Perc.
cresc.
off the string
f
26
27
28
29
30
31
lift
mp
on the string
35
mf legato
on the string
cresc.
Opt.
p
cresc.
mf
32
33
34
35
36
37

43
Vln. 1
Vln. 2
Vla.
Cello
Bass
Harp
Piano
Perc.
off the string
f marcato
off the string
f marcato
off the string
f marcato
off the string
f marcato
f marcato
38
39
40
41
42
43
fp cresc.
fp
fp cresc.
fp cresc.
fp cresc.
fp cresc.
f
f
f
f
44 mp cresc.
45
46 f
47
48
49
04490308

GREENSLEEVES

Sixteenth Century Traditional English
Arranged by BRUCE HEALEY

* Violin 3 (Viola T.C.) part included though not shown on the score.

04490308

29
hi3 4
Solo Vln.
Vln. 1, 2
Vla.
Cello
Bass
Harp
Piano
Perc.
unis.
unis.
unis.
mf
mf
mf
mf
mf
mf
mf
mf
mp
mp
mp
mp
mp
mp
hi4
lift
p
Sus. Cym.
Tri.
Sus. Cym.
Tri.
28
29
30
31
32
33
34
37
Solo Vln.
Vln. 1, 2
Vla.
Cello
Bass
Harp
Piano
Perc.
mf
mf
mf
mf
mf
mf
mf
mf
mf
sim.
sim.
Finger Cym.
35
36
37
mp
38
39
40
41

45
Solo Vln.
Vln. 1, 2
Vla.
Cello
Bass
Harp
Piano
Perc.
unis.
Sus. Cym.
Tri.
Sus. Cym.
42 43 44 mp 45 mf mp 46 47 48 mp
Rit.
dim.
Opt.
unis.
dim.
dim.
dim.
dim.
mf
p
p
p
p
mf
p
Tri.
Mark Tree
49 mf mp 50 51 52 53 54 55 p
04490308
hi3 4
hi4
lift
hi3

DING DONG! MERRILY ON HIGH!

French Carol
Arranged by BRUCE HEALEY

* Violin 3 (Viola T.C.) part included though not shown on the score.

Vln. 1
Vln. 2
Vla.
Cello
Bass
Harp
Piano
Perc.
mf
13   14   15   16   17   18
Vln. 1
Vln. 2
Vla.
Cello
Bass
Harp
Piano
Perc.
19   20   21   22   23   24

Vln. 1
Vln. 2
Vla.
Cello
Bass
Harp
Piano
Perc.
29 div.
mp
Play
mf
f
dim.
mf
f
dim.
mp
f
dim.
mp
f
dim.
mp
f
dim.
mp
Finger Cym.
Bells
25 mf
26
27
28
29 mp
30
Vln. 1
Vln. 2
Vla.
Cello
Bass
Harp
Piano
Perc.
cresc.
Mark Tree
l.v.
31
32
33
34
35
36

37
Vln. 1
mf
Vln. 2
mf
Vla.
mf
Cello
mf
Bass
mf
Harp
mf
Piano
mf
To Timpani (A, D)
Perc.
37
38
39
40
41
43
hi3
hi3
Vln. 1
hi3
hi3
Vln. 2
hi3
lo1
1
Vla.
hi4
2
3
Cello
Bass
Harp
Piano
Perc.
42
43
44
45
46
47

49
hi3
hi3
hi3
hi3
hi3
Vln. 1
Vln. 2
Vla.
Cello
Bass
Harp
Piano
Perc.
f
f
f
f
f
48
49
50
51
52
57
3
3
p
cresc.
p
cresc.
p
cresc.
p
cresc.
p
cresc.
mf
cresc.
f
f
f
f
f
Timp.
p
53
54 cresc.
55
56
57
f

20
04490308
Vln. 1
Vln. 2
Vla.
Cello
Bass
Harp
Piano
Perc.
Bells
Timp.
cresc.

GOD REST YE MERRY, GENTLEMEN
19th Century English Carol
Arranged by BRUCE HEALEY
Espressivo (♩ = 116)
Violin 1
Violin 2
Viola*
Cello
String Bass
Harp (Opt.)
Piano (Opt.)
Percussion (Opt.)
mp
Violin 1
Cello
Vln. 1
Vln. 2
Vla.
Cello
Bass
Harp
Piano
Perc.
Violin 1, 2
Viola
lo1
hi4
hi3
* Violin 3 (Viola T.C.) part included though not shown on the score.
04490308

Vln. 1
Vln. 2
Vla.
Cello
Bass
Harp
Piano
Perc.
Rit.
lo1
lo1
lo2
hi3
hi4
hi4
mp
Bass
13
14
15
16
17
18
19 Faster (♩ = 120)
23
Vln. 1
Vln. 2
Vla.
Cello
Bass
Harp
Piano
Perc.
fp
fp
fp
fp
fp
(V)
(V)
(V)
(V)
off the string
off the string
mf
mf
mf
Play
f l.h. damped
Play
f
mf
Sm. Triangle
p
mf
19
20
21
22
23
24
04490308

Vln. 1
Vln. 2
Vla.
Cello
Bass
Harp
Piano
Perc.
mf
mf
hi4
lift
25
26
27
28
29
30
31
Vln. 1
Vln. 2
Vla.
Cello
Bass
Harp
Piano
Perc.
lo1
hi4
hi4
4
hi4
arco
32
33
34
35
36

Vln. 1
Vln. 2
Vla.
Cello
Bass
Harp
Piano
Perc.
lo1
lo2
4
hi4
fp cresc.
(double strokes opt.)
fp cresc.
(double strokes opt.)
fp cresc.
fp cresc.
fp cresc.
p cresc.
Sus. Cym.
l.v.
fp cresc.
37
38
39
40
41
42
43
(double strokes opt.)
hi3
hi3
hi3
lo2
lo2
lo2
f
f
f
f
f
f
Chimes l.v.
f
44
45
46
47
48
04490308

51
Vln. 1
Vln. 2
Vla.
Cello
Bass
Harp
Piano
Perc.
hi3
hi3
hi3
49
50
51
52
53
59
Vln. 1
Vln. 2
Vla.
Cello
Bass
Harp
Piano
Perc.
lo1
lo1
lo2
lo2
lo2
lo2
lo2
54
55
56
57
58 mf
59 f
60
Sus. Cym.
To Timpani (F#, A, B)

Vln. 1
Vln. 2
Vla.
Cello
Bass
Harp
Piano
Perc.
hi4
61
62
63
64
65
66
67
Accel.
off the string
off the string
cresc.
cresc.
off the string
cresc.
cresc.
ff
ff
ff
ff
ff
8va
cresc.
mf
cresc.
cresc.
ff
Timpani
68
69
70
71 mp
cresc.
72
ff

73 Boldly (♩ = 128)
Vln. 1
Vln. 2
Vla.
Cello
Bass
Harp
Piano
Perc.
marc.
hi3
hi4
hi4
3
3
ff
ff
ff
8va
8va
ff
73
74
75
76
77
81
Vln. 1
Vln. 2
Vla.
Cello
Bass
Harp
Piano
Perc.
f (full bow)
f (full bow)
f (full bow)
f (full bow)
f (full bow)
hi4
3
lift
lift
3
hi3
lo1
Sus. Cym.
l.v.
78
79
80 mf
81 f
82
83
84

Molto Rit.
89
Vln. 1
Vln. 2
Vla.
Cello
Bass
Harp
Piano
Perc.
f   dim.
85   86   87   88   89   90   91
Slower (♩ = 112)
Rit.
Vln. 1
Vln. 2
Vla.
Cello
Bass
Harp
Piano
Perc.
sfz   f   mp
sfz   f   mp
sfz   f   mp
sfz   f   mp
sfz   f   mp
f
mf
f
mp
mf
92 sfz   93 f   94   95   96 p   97 mf
04490308

O COME, ALL YE FAITHFUL
(Adeste Fideles)

Words and Music by JOHN FRANCIS WADE
Latin Words translated by FREDERICK OAKELEY
Arranged by BRUCE HEALEY

* Violin 3 (Viola T.C.) part included though not shown on the score.

Vln. 1
Vln. 2
Vla.
Cello
Bass
Harp
Piano
Perc.
21
hi3
lift
mf
18
19
20
21
22
23
24
25
26
27
Ped.
Ped.
Ped.
Ped.
Ped.
Ped.
Ped.
Ped.
sim.
hi3
hi4
04490308

Vln. 1
Vln. 2
Vla.
Cello
Bass
Harp
Piano
Perc.
29
cresc.
mp
f
33
p
mp
04490308

Vln. 1
Vln. 2
Vla.
Cello
Bass
Harp
Piano
Perc.
f
hi3
piu f
lo2
f
hi3
3
2
hi3
piu f
f
lo1
1
lo1
1
piu f
lo1
f
lo1
lo1
V
piu f
f
piu f
f
piu f
36 mf
37 f
38
39
40 mf
41
Rit.
hi3
3
(V)
lo1
1
(V)
(V)
To Timpani (G,A,D)
Timp.
41 f
42
43 f
44 fp
45 fp

O HOLY NIGHT

French Words by PLACIDE CAPPEAU
English Words by JOHN S. DWIGHT
Music by ADOLPHE ADAM
Arranged by BRUCE HEALEY

* Violin 3 (Viola T.C.) part included though not shown on the score.

14
Vln. 1
Vln. 2
Vla.
Cello
Bass
Harp
Piano
Perc.
hi3
cresc.
lo1 2
cresc.
hi4
13 14 15 16 17 18
23
Vln. 1
Vln. 2
Vla.
Cello
Bass
Harp
Piano
Perc.
mf
hi3
mf
lift
mf
hi4
lo1 1 2 3
mf
mf
mf
Chimes
Sus. Cym.
19 p 20 mp 21 mf 22 p 23 mf 24 25

Vln. 1
Vln. 2
Vla.
Cello
Bass
Harp
Piano
Perc.
31
39
f
cresc.
hi4
Sus. Cym.
Cym. 1st time
Timp. (E, F♯,A,B) 2nd time only
Ped.
Ped.
Ped.
Ped.
Ped.
hi3
hi3
Ped.
Ped.
Ped.
Ped.
Ped.
Ped.
Ped.
26
27
28
29
30
mf
31
f
32
33
34
35
36
37
38
39
04490308

Vln. 1
Vln. 2
Vla.
Cello
Bass
Harp
Piano
Perc.
Rit. 2nd time only
04490308

Vln. 1
Vln. 2
Vla.
Cello
Bass
Harp
Piano
Perc.
1.
2. A Tempo
Rit.
Sus. Cym.
Mark Tree
(Opt.)
04490308

PAT-A-PAN
(Willie, Take Your Drum)

Words and Music by
BERNARD de la MONNOYE
Arranged by BRUCE HEALEY

* Violin 3 (Viola T.C.) part included though not shown on the score.

Vln. 1
Vln. 2
Vla.
Cello
Bass
Harp
Piano
Perc.
hi3
lo2
arco
arco
arco
13
14
15
16
17
18
20
arco
arco
lo1
lo1
lo1
2
lift
lo1
2
3
2
lo1
mf
mf
mf
sim.
mf
mf
mf
mf
19
20
mf
21
22
23
24

Vln. 1
Vln. 2
Vla.
Cello
Bass
Harp
Piano
Perc.
lo1
lo1
3
2 3
25
26
27
28
29
30
33
Opt. Solo
mf marcato
Opt. Solo
mf marcato
4
2
lo1
4
lo1
2 1
Cello
Cello
Viola
Viola
mf
mf
Sus. Cym.
Scrape
mf
31
32
33
34
35
36

Vln. 1
Vln. 2
Vla.
Cello
Bass
Harp
Piano
Perc.
37
38
39
40
41
42
43
Vln. 1
Opt. Solo
Vln. 2
mf   marcato
Vla.
Cello
Bass
Harp
Piano
Triangle
Perc.
43 mf
44
45
46
47
48

All
53
lo2
f marcato
Vln. 1
All
lo1   2   3   lo1 lo2   1   lo2   hi3   All   hi3
Vln. 2
lo1   lo2 2   1 hi3   1   All   f
Vla.
3   4   hi4 1   cresc.   All
Cello
cresc.   All   mf   f
Bass
Play   f
Harp
Play   mf
Piano
Sus. Cym.
Perc.
49   50   51   52 mf   53 f Hand Drum (w/Light Stick) 54

hi3   V
Vln. 1
hi3   V lo2
Vln. 2
>   >   >   2   3   V   V
Vla.
>   2   1   V   V
Cello
>
Bass
>
Harp
Piano
Perc.
55   56   57   58   59   60

Vln. 1
Vln. 2
Vla.
Cello
Bass
Harp
Piano
Perc.
64
piu f
piu f
piu f
piu f
piu f
piu f
piu f
lo2
hi3
hi3
2
Timpani (A,D,E)
f
61
62
63
64
65
66
8va
2
67
68
69
70
71
72
04490308

SILENT NIGHT

Words by JOSEPH MOHR
Translated by JOHN F. YOUNG
Music by FRANZ X. GRUBER
Arranged by BRUCE HEALEY

* Violin 3 (Viola T.C.) part included though not shown on the score.

04490308

46
04490308
Vln. 1
Vln. 2
Vla.
Cello
Bass
Harp
Piano
Perc.
13
mp
(normal)
p
p
p
p
Ped.
Ped.
Ped.
13
14
15
16
17
18
Vln. 1
Vln. 2
Vla.
Cello
Bass
Harp
Piano
Perc.
21
mp
mp
mp
mp
mp
mf
mf
mf
mf
hi4
mf
Ped.
Ped.
Ped.
Ped.
Mark Tree
19
20
21
22
23
24
pp

29
frog
Vln. 1
Vln. 2
Vla.
Cello
Bass
Harp
Piano
Perc.
Opt. Solo
Sus. Cym.
25 26 27 28 29 30 31
37
Vln. 1
Vln. 2
Vla.
Cello
Bass
Harp
Piano
Perc.
Opt. Solo
End Solo
End Solo
32 33 34 35 36 37 38

45
Vln. 1
Vln. 2
Vla.
Cello
Bass
Harp
Piano
Perc.
dim.
cresc.
mp
Ped. Ped. Ped. Ped. Ped. Ped. Ped. Ped.
39 40 41 42 43 44 45
Rit. Rit. frog
lo1 cresc.
cresc.
lo1 cresc.
1
hi4
cresc.
cresc.
f
f
f
f
f
mp
mp
mp
mp
mp
dim.
dim.
dim.
dim.
dim.
dim.
dim.
Sus. Cym. Mark Tree Ped.
Ped. Ped. Ped. Ped.
p mf
46 47 48 49 50 51 52
pp
04490308

CHANUKAH, OY CHANUKAH

* Violin 3 (Viola T.C.) part included though not shown on the score.

04490308

Vln. 1
Vln. 2
Vla.
Cello
Bass
Harp
Piano
Perc.
lo2
lift
pizz.
pizz.
Subito Faster (♩ = 144)
Rit.
lift
lift
arco
arco
normal
lo1
lo2
lo1

24
Vln. 1
Vln. 2
Vla.
Cello
Bass
Harp
Piano
Perc.
Solo, opt.
mf
f
mf
mf
mf
mf
mf
mf
1 3 lo1 2 1 2
1 3 lo1 2 1 2
4
24 25 26 27
Vln. 1
Vln. 2
Vla.
Cello
Bass
Harp
Piano
Perc.
1 lo2 hi3 lift
hi4 1
lift
lift
Shake
28 29 30 31

52
Vln. 1
Vln. 2
Vla.
Cello
Bass
Harp
Piano
Perc.
04490308

Vln. 1
Vln. 2
Vla.
Cello
Bass
Harp
Piano
Perc.
mf
(opt. 8va to bar 61)
(opt. solo)
45

55
04490308

THREE HOLIDAY SONGS

(The Dreydl Song • Jingle Bells • Joy To The World)

Arranged by BRUCE HEALEY

* Violin 3 (Viola T.C.) part included though not shown on the score.

Vln. 1
Vln. 2
Vla.
Cello
Bass
Harp
Piano
Perc.
hi3
lo1
hi3 lo1
1.
2.
"Jingle Bells"
Words and Music by J. PIERPONT
23
p
stacc. sim.
secco
Tacet to m. 39 if Harp is available
Sleigh Bells
hi3
hi4
hi3
hi3
stacc. sim.
stacc. sim.
stacc. sim.
14
15
16
17
18
19
20
21
22
23
24
25
26
27

Vln. 1
Vln. 2
Vla.
Cello
Bass
Harp
Piano
Perc.
hi3
hi4
hi4
31
f
Play
mf
39
f
mf

55
Vln. 1
Vln. 2
Vla.
Cello
Bass
Harp
Piano
Perc.
lift
pizz.
lift
pizz.
mf
lift
pizz. hi3
mf
lift
pizz.
mf
lift
pizz.
mf
mf
hi3
Tacet to m. 71 if Harp is available
p
54
55
56
57
58
59
60
63
Vln. 1
Vln. 2
Vla.
Cello
Bass
Harp
Piano
Perc.
61
62
63
64
65
66
67

72
Vln. 1
Vln. 2
Vla.
Cello
Bass
Harp
Piano
Perc.
arco
arco
arco
arco
arco
Play
Sleigh Bells
lo1
hi3
lo1
1

Vln. 1
Vln. 2
Vla.
Cello
Bass
Harp
mf
Piano
Perc.
80
81
82
83
84
85
86
"Joy To The World"
Words by ISAAC WATTS
Music by GEORGE FRIDERIC HANDEL
88
f
Timp. (A, E)
87
88
f
89
90
91
92

Vln. 1
Vln. 2
Vla.
Cello
Bass
Harp
Piano
Perc.
95
lift
hi4
lo1
hi4
pp
pp
pp
pp
93
94
95
96
97
98
99
lift
mp
mp
mp
mp
pp
mp
f
f
f
f
f
hi3
2
3
2
3
1
1
1.
p
f
mp
99
100
101
102
103
104
105
106
> > > >
> > > >
> > > >
> > > >

04490308

WE WISH YOU A MERRY CHRISTMAS
65
Traditional English Folksong
Arranged by BRUCE HEALEY
Brightly (♩ = 144) or faster
Violin 1
Violin 2
Viola*
Cello
String Bass
Harp (Opt.)
Piano (Opt.)
Percussion (Opt.)
Chimes
l.v.
marc. f
Vln. 1
Vln. 2
Vla.
Cello
Bass
Harp
Piano
Perc.
* Violin 3 (Viola T.C.) part included though not shown on the score.
Copyright © 2003 by HAL LEONARD CORPORATION
International Copyright Secured   All Rights Reserved
04490308

66
Vln. 1
Vln. 2
Vla.
Cello
Bass
Harp
Piano
Perc.
fp
fp
fp
fp
mp
mp
mp
mp
legato
legato
legato
legato
dampen
20
18
19
20
21
22
23
24
25
Vln. 1
Vln. 2
Vla.
Cello
Bass
Harp
Piano
Perc.
28
mf
mf
mf
mf
mf
mf
mf
hi3
hi4
lo1
lo1
2
Sus. Cym.
Sleigh Bells
2
26
27
p
28
mf
29
mp
30
31
32
04490308

Vln. 1
Vln. 2
Vla.
Cello
Bass
Harp
Piano
Perc.
Chimes
36
43
33
34
35
36
37
38
39
40
41
42
43
44
45
46
47
fp
fp
fp
fp
fp
fp
fp
fp
fp
fp
f
f
f
mf
mf
mf
mf
hi3
hi3 hi4
hi3
lo1
hi4
3
2

51
hi3
Vln. 1
mf
Vln. 2
lo1
hi3
mf
lo1
1
Vla.
Cello
Bass
mf
Harp
mf
Piano
Perc.
48
49
50
51
52
53
54
59
Vln. 1
legato
lo2
2
Vln. 2
legato
lo2
2
Vla.
legato
Cello
legato
Bass
legato
Harp
Piano
Sus. Cym.
Perc.
55
56
57
58 mp
59 mf
60
61

67
Vln. 1
Vln. 2
Vla.
Cello
Bass
Harp
Piano
Perc.
f marc.
f marc.
hi3
marc.
f
marc.
f
marc.
f
Sus. Cym.
Sleigh Bells
62 63 64 65 66 67 f 68 mf
Vln. 1
Vln. 2
Vla.
Cello
Bass
Harp
Piano
Perc.
fp
fp
fp
fp
fp
fp
lo1 1 0 hi3 lo2 2
hi4 lo1 1
69 70 71 72 73 74 75

Vln. 1
Vln. 2
Vla.
Cello
Bass
Harp
Piano
Perc.
Timp. (G,A,D)
04490308